I0749841

TRUE WORSHIP:

KNOWING GOD BY DEVELOPING
A CLOSER RELATIONSHIP WITH HIM

TRUE WORSHIP:

KNOWING GOD BY DEVELOPING A CLOSER RELATIONSHIP WITH HIM

(A Roadmap to Find the Relationship with God that He Desires and You Enjoy)

By
Danny E. Davis

Charleston, AR:
COBB PUBLISHING
2018

Published in the United States of America by:

Cobb Publishing
704 E. Main St.
Charleston, AR 72933
www.CobbPublishing.com
CobbPublishing@gmail.com
(479) 747-8372

ISBN: 978-1-947622-30-2

Developing a closer relationship with God (the way God intended) may only be achieved when we understand and diligently engage in true worship.

True worship is feeling with every fiber of your being—heart, spirit, and soul—an overwhelming humility, an awesome amazement, and an overpowering love felt by entering into the presence of the Holy God. It is so overwhelming that one will be brought to tears of joy and a tremendous sense of unworthiness to be in God's presence.

True worship requires you to have a pure heart and to understand God's plan for mankind; the big picture or purpose of the Bible; the nature and attributes of a Holy God; and the importance of spending time alone with God.

True worship in the church requires you to understand how to worship God in spirit (being ever conscious of God's presence and viewing life with Him as center) and in truth (according to the pattern of the New Testament) with a proper (reverent) attitude by preparing your mind to participate in the New Testament pattern of worship.

Once you develop these behaviors and live an obedient life (daily), true worship is continually perfected but never fully achieved and takes place from you to God. As a result, an intimate relationship is developed between you and God. Then God rains down blessings of joy on the worshipper (you) that are only manifest when true worship takes place.

The amount of joy we experience in our relationship with God is directly proportional to the amount of time we invest in worshipping God in spirit and truth and diligently seeking to understand Him.

TABLE OF CONTENTS

Prologue:

"Send out Your light and Your truth;
let them lead me;
Let them bring me to Your holy hill
and to Your dwelling.
Then I will go to the altar of God,
to God my exceeding joy,
And I will praise You with the lyre,
O God, my God."
(Psalm 43:3-4)

Joy in our Relationship with God

Many people today are not happy in their relationship with God, and they have no idea where to begin to make things better. God wants us to have true joy in our relationship with Him. And if our relationship does not bring us joy, it is because we are too busy looking at our feet instead of the God who lights the way and walks with us.

Every relationship that brings us joy requires our active participation and engagement. We get out of relationships what we put into them. Our relationship with God is no different. In order for us to experience joy in our relationship with Him, we must engage God and develop the relationship.

But how?

We need a roadmap to help us on our journey.

> *Godly joy is focused on God. It rejoices in whatever God rejoices about: the accomplishment of His purposes, the triumph of His cause, the redemption of those who have accepted His salvation, and, yes, even the carrying out of His justice.*[1]

Yet I will rejoice in the Lord, I will joy in
the God of my salvation
(Habakkuk 3:18).

Where is God?

Although I had been a Christian for over 26 years, I was not happy with my relationship with God. Something was missing. I knew I was not doing the best I could for Him each day. Some days were good, but some days left me feeling empty in my service. I had become complacent. Where does one start when assessing his spiritual life? Since I did not have the answers I needed, I thought it would be best to ask God. He assures us if we will *diligently* seek Him, we will find Him.

"But if from there you seek the Lord your
God, you will find Him if you seek Him with
all your heart and with all your soul."
(Deuteronomy 4:29)

---

[1] Gary Henry, https://wordpoints.com/godly-joy-november-6/

Seek God with all my heart and soul—but what does that mean? How does one do that? Those were the words God told Moses to tell the Israelites. The Bible is filled with examples of God's Holy Spirit telling God's servants how to find Him. I knew the emptiness in my relationship with God was not God's fault – it was mine.

I began to ponder how to find more fulfillment in my relationship. I knew God was aware of just how empty I felt in my present circumstances. And then I read a verse that has become one of my favorites. It told me that I needed to do something, to fill that void of my empty relationship with God and seek Him more diligently, because He is looking for the people who earnestly strive to seek Him.

"The Lord looks down from heaven on all mankind to see if there are any who understand, any who seek God." (Psalm 14:2)

No doubt that confirms God was perfectly doing His part so I could have a better relationship with Him. But what did God mean in this verse when we read He was looking down to "see if there are any who understand?" "Understand what?" I wondered. More on this thought in the chapter on "The Importance of Understanding."

So I began to wonder where I should start in developing a closer relationship with God. One that would bring contentment. One where I knew I was giving it my all and doing my best.

Setting Aside Time to Pray and Meditate

I knew I could pray about doing my part to have a better relationship, and He would answer my prayers. I also knew I needed to set aside a lot of quiet and solitary time to meditate. Meditate? No, I am not writing about that new-age nonsense so prevalent today but which cannot fill the void in our lives—that only God can fill. My definition of "meditate" is to "focus clearly and sharply" on a thought. Making a clear, conscious effort to focus on what was missing in my relationship. *That* was what I needed. What was I doing wrong? How could I find more fulfillment in my walk with Him?

Understanding the Bible's Big Picture

After much prayerful consideration and thought, I realized I could have a closer, more-fulfilling relationship with God if I could understand the big picture of the Bible. How many times have you attended church, and the focus was on a topic or a chapter or a verse of the Bible? Don't get me wrong, there is nothing wrong with teaching in this manner; however, I was never taught the Bible's big picture. I needed to see the forest before I saw the trees. I needed to see the strategic picture of the Bible and then I could understand the books, chapters, and verses.

In my former profession, I traveled and moved every couple of years but no matter how many local churches I had attended, no one had ever explained the big picture of the Bible. So I prayed:

Lord, God Almighty,

Thou knowest my heart and Thou knowest my longing, my desire to come into a deeper relationship with Thee. Father, in humility I pray, show me the big picture of the Bible. Allow me to understand it well enough that I may teach others and glorify Thee. Lord, I want to worship Thee in spirit and truth and have a closer relationship with Thee. Please, Lord, show me the way.

In Jesus' name, amen.

Waiting on the Lord

I do not remember how long had passed, but perhaps a few months later, I walked into a bookstore, and I proceeded to the area on religion where I found a book on the "big picture" of the Bible. I stood in awe examining the pages of that book—awestruck and utterly amazed that God had answered my prayer. I knew at that moment that my life would change forever. I told God I would teach others and draw closer to Him because He had answered my prayer. I kept my word and He kept His word to a diligent seeker – He answered!

Living in the Presence of God

The ability to see the Bible from a strategic or big-picture perspective was what I needed to break through my stagnation and develop a deeper relationship with God. I put together an intense study, and I taught Bible classes on the big picture for over a year after that incident. That study allowed me to learn true worship to God—as an individual and in the assembly. I will never be the same and neither will my walk with God.

As a result of that study, I began to understand the importance of reading the Bible for understanding, and not solely to gain knowledge. I will elaborate further on this in another chapter. Additionally, and perhaps most importantly, I began to see God more clearly from His Word. I began to see His nature and attributes, His plan for mankind, and the importance of spending time developing my relationship with Him.

As I began to draw closer to God, I learned the meaning of true worship as an individual and as one participating in the assembly. My attitude about God came into a much clearer focus. Reflecting on God's holiness, which is the foundation for all of His many attributes, allowed me to properly prepare my mind to worship God the way He desires: in spirit and in truth. Although I have always followed the New Testament pattern of worship in order to be in a right relationship with God, **I began to see the difference between doctrine and spirituality.** *I began to worship God by focusing on God instead of by focusing on my actions and imperfections from a "checklist."* ***I began to***

"know" God instead of just "knowing about" Him. Do not get me wrong, following God according to His plan (doctrine) is necessary; however, once you develop a true pursuit of God and worship Him in Spirit, your doctrinal actions will flow much easier and without thought. Your focus will be on God and how to please Him, how to find out more about Him. My worship in the assembly became more focused because my individual efforts were more focused. It has made all the difference.

I have grown more spiritually in the last couple of years than I have grown in the preceding 26 years combined as a Christian. I am deeply saddened that it took me so many decades to understand true worship to the Holy God of heaven and earth. However, I am eternally grateful to Jesus for extending His grace to allow me to find what I have found, because this kind of relationship with God is not taught in churches today. Men have failed to proclaim what the Bible teaches about worshipping God in spirit and truth.

And because of many discussions I had with other Christians, about how to develop an intimate, closer relationship with God, I felt compelled to share this roadmap with all who are seeking to learn true worship—worship that develops a closer walk with God. If you are searching for a more fulfilling relationship with God, one where you are closer to Him than ever before, you have found a roadmap. This plan will point you to God the Father; Jesus the Son, the Holy Spirit, and to the Bible. Now you can *know* God intimately instead of just knowing *about* Him.

Before I share the roadmap, however, it is necessary to establish the correct definition of "true worship" or "knowing" God.

There are many definitions floating around these days. For example, an evangelist and author, Derek Prince, who emerged from the worldwide charismatic movement of the '60s and '70s, claimed "true worship" is "attitude that follows after praise and thanksgiving from Christians have taken place."[2] His definition is very shallow, and the roadmap he provides is vague. Prince maintains "God has given us a model that will lead us into worship, and therefore His presence. This model is the tabernacle."[3] Prince uses the tabernacle of the Old Testament to symbolically explain how we enter into the presence of God today. I believe his focus is too narrow, and his book is too theoretical to ever prove it will lead someone to experience true worship within themselves and within the assembly. How could one measure whether true worship had taken place by this definition and this roadmap? This definition weakens his arguments, and his conclusions about a roadmap to enter into the presence of God are incorrect.

On the other hand, there is a well-known author and evangelist who preached on deeply spiritual topics in the early twentieth century, and he has a very

---

[2] Prince, Entering the Presence of God, 21.
[3] *Ibid.,* 51.

thoughtful definition of true worship that is worth considering.

Dr. Aiden W. Tozer maintained:

> *"(True) worship is to feel in your heart and express in some appropriate manner a humbling but delightful sense of admiring awe, astonished wonder, and overpowering life in the presence of that most ancient Mystery, that Majesty which philosophers call the First Cause, but which we call our Father in Heaven."*[4]

I can relate to this definition and to Tozer's sense of worship. However, I am concerned that there is no way to know for certain some of the things that Tozer wrote about God. That would scare me personally, based on God's condemnation of Job's three friends in Job 42:7 for not speaking the truth about God. One must be careful in speaking of God. Another difference between Tozer's book and this one is that Tozer does not provide a roadmap for how to achieve a more personal, joyful relationship with God.

Finally, there is another well-known and respected author, J. I. Packer, who provides a definition of "true worship," and that definition is simply "knowing God." Packer's book is a fantastic read on gaining a better relationship with God; however, my conclusions about having a more personal relationship with God are very different from his. Packer maintains that hav-

---

[4] Snyder, cited in Tozer: Mystery of the Holy Spirit, 7-8.

ing a more personal relationship with God comes about by "one day waking up to the fact that God is actually speaking to you – you! – through the biblical message."[5] This doesn't just happen. You don't just wake up and have a more personal relationship with God. I maintain one must agonize or distress about their relationship with God or it will never change. God is the same (immutable) towards the people who desire Him. Therefore, it is incumbent upon the seeker to engage and take an active role to develop his relationship with God. You don't just wake up to "true worship" or truly "knowing" God. Having the relationship with God that He desires and you enjoy doesn't come about by accident. I maintain it comes from a pure heart, which must constantly be guarded, refined, and worked on by the owner and by God. Another difference between Packer's book, *Knowing God*, and my book is the roadmap to get you to "true worship" or in Packer's terms "knowing God."

Packer provides the following roadmap:

> *"First, listening to God's Word and receiving it as the Holy Spirit interprets it, in application to oneself; second, noting God's nature and character, as His Word works to reveal it; third, accepting His invitations and doing what He commands; fourth, recognizing and rejoicing in the*

---

[5] J.I. Packer, Knowing God, 36.

love He has shown in thus approaching you and drawing you into this divine fellowship."[6]

This is totally different than the conclusions to which I have come regarding the roadmap to true worship. I do agree God's nature must be sought and God must be the primary focus, but I disagree with Packer's other points in his roadmap.

I maintain true worship stems from those with a pure heart, who seek out God's nature and attributes to learn more of Him. The true worshipper understands God's plan for mankind, the big picture of the Bible, and the importance of spending time alone with God. This individual roadmap will open up true worship by the individual in the assembly and allow a person to understand a more satisfying relationship with God. Finally, this roadmap requires constant engagement and an obedient life if one wants to continue honing their relationship with God, because the relationship on our part will never be perfected—but it is not like work at all – it is a joyful and an extremely fulfilling path. The way God intended.

Based on the preceding conclusions about authors who have written on this topic and for the purposes of this paper, I define "true worship" as follows.

[6] Ibid, 37.

Definition of True Worship

True worship is to feel with every fiber of your being (heart, spirit, and soul) an overwhelming humility, an awesome amazement, and an overpowering love enjoyed by entering into the presence of the Holy God. It is so overwhelming that one will be brought to tears of joy and a tremendous sense of unworthiness to be in God's presence. That is my definition of true worship. If you follow the roadmap contained in the following pages, you will develop a personal relationship with God and be "on fire" in diligently pursuing His ways. If this is your aim, God bless you in your efforts.

"True worship" or "knowing God" is about having a growing, personal, intimate relationship with Him, an ever-mindful consciousness of God's presence through which you make daily decisions and interact with others. God becomes the center of life! God is put first in all things.

Viewing the world with God as your center will never be perfected – it must be renewed daily – but it is not burdensome to seek God daily. It is a joy. The diligent seeker daily renews his passion for God. God is his top priority!

Diligently seeking God by following this roadmap will lead to true worship (knowing God), which will lead to a personal relationship with God. This will lead you to worship God as He desires, resulting in more joy and fulfillment than anything you will ever experience in this world – the way God intended. This method will put you on a path to hunger and thirst for God daily, the way David did in Psalm 63.

My prayers are with you as you diligently seek to truly worship the Lord by developing a closer relationship with Him… the relationship He desires to have with you.

May God be glorified!

1
Understanding the Importance of Preparing Your Heart (spirit and soul)

"Blessed are the pure in heart,
for they shall see God!"
(Matthew 5:8)

The pure in heart shall see God's face. If the thought of seeing God's face does not excite you, then you do not have a pure heart and you do not have the relationship with God that He desires. I suspect you desire a pure heart; otherwise, you would not be reading this right now. Or you may have a pure heart, but you are working on perfecting your humility before God.

I have often wondered why some people obey God; some consider it, but put it off for a more convenient time (like King Agrippa); and some have no desire whatsoever for God (which leads to a continual void in their heart that they will try to fill with the worship of worldly things). I have come to the conclusion the difference is people who diligently seek God have a pure heart for godly things, and the ones who do not seek God do not have a pure heart for godly things. It all goes back to the heart. If you have a pure heart, guard it to make sure only godly things enter into it. It takes daily work—one never arrives at a state of accomplished perfection. If you do not have a pure heart, or you have a heart that you desire to be more pure, then read carefully.

Definition of the heart (spirit and soul)

There is much confusion about how to define the heart. For purposes of our study, the heart consists of *the intellect (mind/conscience), emotions, and will of a person.* The heart is that part of a person which allows him *to think [intellect (mind/conscience)], to feel (emotions), and to act (will).* Human beings contain a heart, spirit, soul, and body.

"The spirit is the element in humanity that gives us the ability to have an intimate relationship with God. Whenever the word 'spirit' is used, it refers to the immaterial part of humanity that 'connects' with God, who Himself is a Spirit."[1] John 4:24 informs us that God is Spirit.

"The soul is the life essence of the body that is removed at the time of physical death."[2] There is an example of this description in Genesis 35:18 and Jeremiah 15:2.

A man's entire being (heart, spirit, and soul) is important to God but the essence of a person begins in the heart. This is why we are told in Proverbs 4:23 to "Above all else, guard your heart, for everything you do flows from it."

---

[1] Got Questions: Difference Between Soul and Spirit
[2] *Ibid.*

Halting any form of evil from entering your mind and conscience is critical to having a pure heart and being "spiritually alive" in Christ (1 Corinthians 2:11; Hebrews 4:12; James 2:26). The scriptures tell us that only true believers are spiritually alive (that is, ever conscious of God's presence and viewing life's decisions with Him as center) and able to have an intimate relationship with Him. Please stop and consider or meditate on this sentence for a while: only true believers are spiritually alive and able to have an intimate relationship with God.

Many people live for doctrine, while they are spiritually sleeping—thinking they're alive in Christ when they're really dead to Him (Revelation 3:1; 2:2-5; 1 Corinthians 11:29-20). Notice I wrote dead "to" Christ and not dead "in" Christ; this is because the spiritually dead are not "in" Christ (Ephesians 2:1-5 and Colossians 2:13).

Does the thought that "only true believers are spiritually alive" mean you are not a true believer if you are spiritually dead? Let God answer that for us—the Scriptures tell us only true believers are spiritually alive (1 Corinthians 2:11; Hebrews 4:12; and James 2:26. Complacency is the ruin of many Christians. Do not be complacent or content with your relationship with God – diligently seek His face daily!

If you are a true believer, but you feel spiritually dead because you have no joy in your relationship with God, this is your roadmap to fix your death and come alive spiritually. Start with a pure heart.

What is a Pure Heart?

People with pure hearts are ***uncompromising*** in their efforts to put God first and love Him with all of their heart, soul, and strength. This is difficult for new Christians, and often for mature Christians too; however, as we grow in our relationship with God, and joy becomes prevalent, at some point we will experience a "tipping point" where diligently seeking God becomes our priority. And the joy we experience will be like no other feeling on this earth—the joy of feeling doctrinally and spiritually alive in God. But none of this is possible without a pure heart.

Pray for a Pure Heart

Perhaps the very first thing you need to do to have a joyful relationship with God is to pray for a pure heart. But please be sure of your request, because if you are sincere, it may turn your life upside down as God creates a pure heart in you. Do not ask God to give you a pure heart if you do not mean it. And by that you must have made a total commitment to begin putting God first in your life, regardless of your circumstances. If you are ready for no compromise in the LORD, pray:

> *Most holy, Father God, Lord, You know I am not content in my relationship with Thee. Lord, please create in me a clean heart, O LORD, purify me in my ways and allow me to experience the joy in my relationship with You that*

You intended for me to experience. I am ready to make You the center of my life and put You first in all things. Lord, please, create in me a pure heart so that I may serve Thee more diligently and give You my best. In Jesus' name I humbly make this plea. Amen.

When you pray this prayer, or one in your own words, don't stop until you see your life change and God is coming into focus in your life. Then rejoice in gladness as God answers your prayers. He will give you the desires of your heart, provided your heart is ready to be purified. If you need encouragement, consider God's servant David – a man who God proclaimed was after His own heart.

David Prayed for a Pure Heart

David probably wrote over half of the Psalms. Did he have a pure heart? David fell short a lot in God's eyes, but he also poured out his heart before God, acknowledged his sin, got up, and worked harder to serve God. David poured out his heart to God in some of the most beautiful words ever written.

Hide Your face from my sins,
and blot out all my iniquities.
Create in me a clean heart, O God
and renew a right spirit within me
Do not cast me away from your presence,
and do not take your Holy Spirit from me
(Psalm 51:9-11)

Search me, O God, and know my heart;
try me, and know my thoughts,
and see if there is any wicked way in me,
and lead me in the everlasting way.

I would also recommend Psalm 145 as a beautiful example of David's praise for God.

Even with all of his shortcomings and egregious sins, God still proclaimed David "a man after His heart" in 1 Samuel 13:14. Let us pursue God without compromise, work hard to please God, and ask in humility that we would be people after God's own heart. What a worthwhile goal in this life!

2
Understanding God's Nature and Attributes

"This is what the LORD says:
'Let not the wise boast of their wisdom or the strong boast of their strength or the rich boast of their riches, but let the one who boasts boast about this: that they have the understanding to know Me, that I am the LORD, who exercises kindness, justice, and righteousness on earth, for in these I delight,' declares the LORD."
(Jeremiah 9:23-24)

God desires if anyone should boast, they boast about having the understanding to know Him. The point is God wants us to come to a knowledge of Him. That is more important than boasting about wisdom, strength, and riches. This is important to God; and it must be important to us.

Since *knowing* God is so important, we ought to get to know Him through His nature, His attributes, and seek the highest ways to think about Him.

When you think about God, what comes to mind? The thoughts you have of Him will determine your attitude and relationship with Him. We cannot comprehend God, and our thoughts of Him have been tainted by the things of this world. For example, we have no description of what Jesus looked like when He walked on this earth, but your mind instantly conjures up a Jesus who looks like the paintings or drawings you've seen. Do you really think it does the Lord justice when our picture of Him is based on paint instead of power, on drawings instead of deity? It is not wise to put false ideas of God the Father, Jesus the Son, or the Holy Spirit into our minds. So how do we remove from our minds any images or thoughts of God that would lessen who He is? How do we form the highest and loftiest possible thoughts of God so we can have a proper attitude toward Him?

First, we need to pray that God would allow us to see who He is more clearly from His word. Pray earnestly with a sincere heart to know God more intimately, and He will answer your prayers. *Second*, we need to actively replace the false thoughts or images we may have of God with thoughts of Him from His word.

The Holiness of God

The nature of God is holiness. *"Holiness is the unique aspect of God's nature that is without parallel anywhere else in the universe."*[1] It is very difficult to define "holiness," because we have no comprehension of God's true nature; however, it appears that holiness

---

[1] Prince, Set Apart for God, 13.

may be the foundation for all of God's other attributes. It may be all that God is in purity, perfection, and majesty.

There are two visions in the Bible where God is referred to as "holy" three times consecutively. This is a great place to start putting images in your mind about God. Again, the goal is to read the Bible and replace the man-made images or thoughts you have of God with thoughts of God from His holy Word. Isaiah chapter 6 reveals a vision that Isaiah had, of God sitting on His throne, the train of His robe filling the temple. Heavenly beings, seraphim, cried out to God, proclaiming "Holy, holy, holy is the LORD." When he saw this vision, when he saw the Holiness of God, Isaiah realized how impure and imperfect he was.

"In the year that King Uzziah died, I saw the Lord sitting on a throne, high and lifted up, and the train of His robe filled the temple.: Above it stood seraphim; each one had six wings: with two he covered his face, with two he covered his feet, and with two he flew.: And one cried to another and said: "Holy, holy, holy is the LORD of hosts; The whole earth is full of His glory!" And the posts of the door were shaken by the voice of him who cried out, and the house was filled with smoke. So I said: "Woe is me, for I am undone! Because I am a man of unclean lips, And I dwell in the midst of a people of unclean lips; For my eyes have

seen the King, The LORD of hosts."
(Isaiah 6:1-5)

We read of a similar event in the book of Revelation, where heavenly creatures of which we have never seen any comparison proclaim the holiness and majesty of God.

"The four living creatures, each having six wings, were full of eyes around and within. And they do not rest day or night, saying: "Holy, holy, holy, Lord God Almighty, Who was and is and is to come!" Whenever the living creatures give glory and honor and thanks to Him who sits on the throne, who lives forever and ever, the twenty-four elders fall down before Him who sits on the throne and worship Him who lives forever and ever, and cast their crowns before the throne, saying: 'You are worthy, O Lord, To receive glory and honor and power; For You created all things, And by Your will they exist and were created.'"
(Revelation 4:8-11)

I recommend you review other passages in the Bible, which inform us of God's holiness (Psalm 69:9, Isaiah 57:15, and Revelation 51:4 are some). Meditate and pray on the verses, and ask God to bring you into a better comprehension of and respect for His holiness. When you spend time seeking to understand His holiness, you lay a foundation to gain understanding of God's many other attributes.

Our Response to God's Holiness

Our response to God's holiness should be one of extreme humbleness. When we begin to understand more of God's nature, we will understand we are not worthy to enter into His presence – just as Isaiah experienced. Isaiah immediately realized how unclean or impure he was when He saw a vision of the holy God.

So how do we reconcile this proclamation from Peter, if we are impure in God's eyes?

"But just as He who called you is holy, so be holy in all you do; for it is written: 'Be holy, because I am holy'" (1 Peter 1:15-16).

We are only made holy in God's sight because of the blood sacrifice of Jesus. This sacrifice covers us when we sin and fall short; however, as Christians, we have an obligation to be obedient to God, serving Him to the best of our ability (Ephesians 2:10, James 2:24-26). Our diligent work to live a life of obedience (in doctrine and spirit) plus the sacrifice of Jesus is the closest we can get on earth to being holy. When we sin, as long as we repent and rededicate ourselves to obedience, then the blood of Jesus covers our sins and keeps us holy in the sight of God (1 John 1:7-9). There are some who believe that Jesus's sacrifice will cover mankind even if they continue to *willingly* sin and disobey God; however, this false doctrine (called *Universalism*) is a deception of the devil.

> *For if we sin willfully, after having received a knowledge of the truth, there remains no more sacrifice for sins, but a fearful looking expectation of judgment and fiery indignation which will devour the adversaries (Hebrews 10:26-27).*

In order for our relationship with God to bring joy for us and glory to Him, there must be mutual engagement. God will keep His Word perfectly to us; we have a responsibility to do our best for Him and not take advantage of His grace (Romans 6:1-2; 1 Peter 2:16).

Attributes (Meditations on verses about God)

As mentioned previously, J. I. Packer and A.W. Tozer have written extensively on the nature and attributes of God. They listed attributes and expounded upon them. However, a list would not do justice to inform you about God, because it would not adequately articulate His being. Instead, I want to share with you a simple exercise that will increase your knowledge of God's nature and attributes in a way that will allow you to meditate on Him and continue a diligent pursuit – especially from the Bible – to understand Him better. By doing so, you will be drawn into a better, more intimate relationship.

Begin in the book of Genesis, and every time you come to a verse that tells about God's nature and attributes, highlight that verse in a specific color. Once you go through the book and highlight all the verses in this category, take the time to meditate on them and focus on understanding them more diligently. Complete this exercise for every book in the Bible when you read something unique about the Holy Spirit and His ways.

As an example, I personally highlighted a few unique verses about God from my readings in the book of Genesis.

The first verse I highlighted for further contemplation was the second verse in the Bible. Just imagine the Spirit of God hovering above the face of the waters before He created the land. Now consider the implications. When I first read this, my mind thought about God's presence being perhaps a few feet by a few feet. But to limit God in this way is an example of how we need to better form our impressions of Him. This verse tells us His Spirit was hovering above the waters – this could mean His Spirit is so magnificent that He was hovering over every single inch of the waters. This is an example of how we should not contain God.

"The earth was without form, and void;
and darkness was on the face of the deep.
And the Spirit of God was hovering over
the face of the waters."
(Genesis 1:2)

God is Spirit, and in the next passage we consider, try to imagine the Spirit of God "walking" in the garden in the cool of the day. Imagine how blessed Adam and Eve were to be in the presence of God! Shortly after Adam and Eve sinned, God removed Himself from their presence and removed them from the Garden of Eden. We have been trying to get back into God's presence since man's fall. I often think about that when I read this verse.

"And they heard the sound of the LORD God walking in the garden in the cool of the day, and Adam and his wife hid themselves from the presence of the LORD God among the trees of the garden."
(Genesis 3:8)

The next verse I highlighted is interesting to me because God says the man has become like one of "Us." "Us" must refer to the triune nature of God: the Father, the Son, and the Holy Spirit. This verse is also interesting because God warns that man might put out his hand to eat of the tree of life and live forever. Oh, someday won't it be joyful when Jesus returns and takes His saints back to God, at which time we can all eat freely from the tree of life. What an amazing thought!

"Then the LORD God said, 'Behold, the man has become like one of Us, to know good and evil. And now, lest he put out his

hand and take also of the tree of life,
and eat, and live forever.'"
(Genesis 3:22)

Following the above examples will greatly benefit you in seeking to understand God's nature and attributes. The Bible alone contains all the information we will ever need to obtain the relationship with God that He desires and we enjoy – the way God intended for man's relationship with Him to be.

3
The Importance of Understanding (and Diligently Seeking)

"The Lord looks down from heaven on all mankind to see if there are any who understand, any who seek God."
(Psalm 14:2)

The Difference between Knowledge and Understanding

I am always amazed when I hear people tell me they have read the Bible cover to cover for the "umpteenth" time this year. I am amazed when I ask them what they learned. Rarely, does anyone rant and rave about a deeper understanding of the Bible, of God or of His expectations for mankind. The reason this excitement of having read the Bible again is so rare for so many people is because they do not understand what they read. There is a tremendous difference in reading to gain *knowledge* and reading to gain *understanding.*

The book of Proverbs informs us of the value of wisdom and the difference between knowledge and understanding.

"My son, if you receive My Words, and treasure My commands with you, so you incline your ear to wisdom, and apply your

heart to understanding; Yes, if you cry out for discernment, and lift up your voice for understanding, If you seek her as silver, and search for her as for hidden treasures; Then you will understand the fear of the Lord, and find the knowledge of God. For the Lord gives wisdom; from His mouth come knowledge and understanding; He stores up sound wisdom for the upright... then you will understand righteousness and justice, equity and every good path. When wisdom enters your heart, and knowledge is pleasant to your soul, Discretion will preserve you; understanding will keep you. (Proverbs 2:1-12)

Verse two recommends action: "applying your heart to understanding." We must take an active role to make sense of what we read in the Bible. Don't just read a verse that you don't understand and move on to the next verse for the sake of reading. Use Bible study tools to assist you if you don't understand the intent of the word, verse, or concept. Verse three indicates we should earnestly seek to understand. In other words, it may take critical thought to figure out the meaning, but don't give up searching for the meaning. Remain diligent. Verse four provides us with a comparison to which the majority of people in this world can relate: seek to understand God's Word as if it were silver. Many people can relate to searching and seeking wealth or treasure. A lot of people have sacrificed their lives in search of wealth. *What have we sacrificed to understand the Bible and the commandments of God?* Verse five says we can understand the proper way to worship, true worship to God in a way that will bring us closer to Him. Skip down to verse nine, which tells us we can expect to learn about the character and attributes (one of the tenants of true worship) of God, if we will diligently seek to understand.

Foundation for a Truly Intimate Relationship with God

Please pay attention to what you have just read about the importance of seeking to understand God's Word with all your might. Meditate and pray on this thought! Displaying proper effort, along with a pure heart, are the ***beginning*** of having a truly remarkable and joyful experience in your service to God. Are you up to this task? Are you ready to work to improve your relationship with Him? Your life on earth will be meaningless if you do not. Your life will be one of vainly trying to fill the void in your heart which was meant to be filled with a meaningful relationship with the Creator. On the other hand, if you will take heed to Proverbs 2 and apply yourself to understanding God's laws, statutes, and judgments, then you will have more ***joy*** on this planet than you ever thought possible – yes, even during times of trials and tribulations. You will experience the joy for which you were created:

"The prospect of the righteous is joy, but the hopes of the wicked comes to nothing" (Proverbs 10:28).

And you will allow God to simultaneously receive the glory due His name. The glory He deserves from His creation as written in Revelation 4:11 –

"You are worthy, our Lord and God, to receive glory and honor and power, for You created all things, and by Your will they were created and have their being."

4
Understanding God's Plan for Mankind

God wants a family! He wants His creation – mankind – to worship Him in our current form (heart, spirit, and soul) and in the form (spirit) we will become when we meet a physical death. God has a spiritual kingdom of servants who were and are obedient. He wants us to be overly joyed when we worship Him so He may be glorified as He deserves. God intended for His people to be with Him forever in heaven from the foundation of the world, but the devil tried (and failed) to disrupt those plans.

In Genesis 1:31, we read how "God saw all that He had made, and it was very good." However, by Genesis 3, we see the devil introduced sin to Adam and Eve. Therefore, the devil brought evil into the world between Genesis 1:31 and Genesis 3. It is generally accepted that Satan was originally created as an angel, given freedom of choice by God. The devil chose to rebel and sin and introduced sin to Adam and Eve. God also made Adam and Eve with freedom of choice, and they chose to sin as well. Sin is the transgression or breaking of God's law. They chose to break God's law and set the tone for mankind and God's plan for redemption.

In chapter two of this book, you read about God's nature and attributes. The foundation of God, His nature, is holiness. God in His holiness is pure, perfect, and set apart. When Adam and Eve sinned in the Garden, they were separated from God because of His holiness. God had to separate Himself from them and deal with them because of His nature and attributes. Since He is a God of justice, a penalty had to be paid for the sin Adam and Eve committed. That penalty had to be in the form of a sacrifice. The shedding of blood is the sacrifice.

"For the life of the flesh is in the blood, and I have given it to you upon the altar to make atonement for your souls; for it is the blood that makes atonement for your sou." (Leviticus 17:11).

Even though man sinned against God, God in His graciousness allowed man an opportunity to continue in a relationship with Him by sacrificing animals (under the Old Testament Law, which is now null and void because of Christ's perfect sacrifice).

By the time we get to Genesis 12, God chose a man, through whom Jesus (a perfect blood sacrifice) would come, to allow all of mankind to be in a right relationship with Him. Abraham was chosen, because of his obedience and faithfulness to God, to be the great ancestor through whom came the Israelites, who would proclaim Jehovah to the nations. God also expected the Israelites to be obedient to Him.

From the time of Abraham, and throughout the Old Testament, we read stories of the Israelites (some were faithful, but most were not). We read about God and how He expects His people to worship Him in spirit and truth. We read about God's wrath, mercy, justice, love, majesty, His holiness and many other attributes. We find why there is a need for redemption, how God built an earthly nation of followers to obey Him and proclaim Him to other nations. As God built the nation of Israelites and the people multiplied, God educated His people about the importance of worshipping Him properly. When the Israelites were obedient, they prospered; and when they were disobedient, they did not prosper. The same holds true today for God's people.

God disciplined, refined, and punished the Israelites to make them closer to His image of how they should be. And then Jesus came.

When God was ready, in the fullness of time, Jesus came through the lineage of Abraham through one of the twelve tribes of Israel – Judah. The specifics of Jesus's coming were important because God had informed the prophets, who told the people about them.

Jesus came from heaven to serve as a perfect blood sacrifice to bear the sins of all mankind.

When Jesus died and shed His blood, He made a way for all mankind to be in a right relationship with God.

In the current age, we have a full understanding of what we need to do to be in a right relationship with God. We have the Bible, which gives us the blueprint for the relationship God wants us to have with Him.

Under the Old Testament, when God's people were disobedient and sinful, the high priest would offer a sacrifice for the people once a year to atone for their sins. When Jesus died on the cross, the old law was fulfilled and a new covenant between God and man came into existence.

Under the New Testament covenant, people may enter into a right relationship by being baptized (a complete water submersion) for the remission, or washing away, of sins. When you are baptized, you enter into the death, burial, and resurrection of Jesus. After baptism, God expects you to be obedient and to live set apart from the world. The problem is no matter how hard we try "all have sinned and fall short of the glory of God" (Romans 3:23). When a man sins, he must "repent" or change his heart, regretting he committed the sin, and live daily in attempt to avoid sin as much as possible. Repentance comes about by having a remorseful attitude or grieving disappointment at having committed sin (2 Corinthians 7:10).

If you continue steadfast in your walk with God, you will have the joy at growing in your relationship with God. As you diligently seek God and grow in your relationship, your joy will increase with each passing day.

There will be temptations from the devil (1 Peter 5:8), God will test you (2 Chronicles 32:31), and time and chance happen to all (Ecclesiastes 9:11), but you will have comfort in God. He who maintains obedience to God even to the point of death (Revelation 2:10) will receive eternal life and dwell in God's house forever to see His face.

God created us to glorify Him and enjoy doing so. This is God's plan for mankind.

5
Understanding the Big Picture of the Bible

As I wrote in the prologue, understanding the big picture of the Bible was critical for me, and it became the missing link that led me to find more and more insights about God that shaped my personal relationship with Him. In the majority of churches that meet on the first day of the week, I would dare say most of those churches neither teach nor understand the importance of the big picture of the Bible. How can one truly understand the Bible unless they understand the purpose behind why it was written and what the entire story is all about? This chapter aims to open your eyes to see God's big plan from His holy Word. My prayer is that it will allow you to see the Bible in ways that you have never considered, and as a result, you will better glorify God.

Big Picture Outline

In keeping with my intent to teach you the strategic outline or big picture, I want to share with you the Bible's big picture outline, broken down by a prologue, 6 chapters, and an epilogue—twenty major Biblical events, and the books of the Bible associated with the major events (with approximate dates). This will provide you with a roadmap as we examine on the twenty major events in more detail. Again, the entire point of outlining the Bible from this strategic perspective is to give you a comprehensive understanding of God's plan for mankind.

INTRODUCTION

The Bible was written over the course of 1,500 years by over 40 authors in three different languages (Hebrew, Greek and some Aramaic), yet few understand its big-picture purpose. It provides us the story of how we came into existence, and our purpose on this earth. God created us as worshipful beings, which means we all worship something. Jesus said, "Where your treasure is, there your heart will be also" (Matthew 6:21). Those who know the story of God and why He created mankind have the best chance to be fulfilled in this life with true purpose and joy. Seeking to understand this story will bring us the joy God intended for us – if we seek it diligently – and it will simultaneously glorify God.

This layout focuses on the big picture from a spiritual perspective (God's spiritual plans for us) as well as from a historical perspective. It is important you understand both to develop a fuller, more meaningful relationship with God. Understanding the historical layout will simultaneously allow you to grow spiritually and by doing so, your relationship with God will become closer than ever before.

I am indebted to *The Holman QuickSource Guide to Understanding the Bible: A Book-by-Book Overview* by Kendell H. Easley. This was the book that, in answer to my prayers, God brought into my life to help me understand the big picture of the Bible. It started me on the current path of true worship.

ONE SENTENCE SUMMARY

If someone asked you to explain the Bible in one sentence, what would you say? Many people may have a hard time stating it succinctly. I propose to you that the entire story of the Bible can be summed up in this sentence:

> *The Lord God through His Christ is graciously building a kingdom of redeemed people for their joy and for His own glory.*

CHAPTERS

If someone asked you to break the Bible down into chapters, where would you start? The following summary will provide you with a big-picture overview of the Bible. Please note: the dates given are educated guesses. The point of this section is not to tell you "this is exactly when it happened," but to give you the overview, and a very close estimation of the year(s) in which the events took place.

Big Picture Summary Bible Outline[1]

ONE SENTENCE SUMMARY:

[1] The one-sentence summary, prologue, chapters, and epilogue were taken from Holman's QuickSource Guide to Understanding the Bible – A Book-by-Book Overview.

The Lord God through His Christ is graciously building a kingdom of redeemed people for their joy and for His own glory.

***Prologue: Need For Redemption (4004–2091 BC)*[2]**

GEN 1-11

1. Creation
    a. Genesis 1-5
2. Fall of Man
    a. Genesis 3
3. Flood
    a. Genesis 6-9
4. Scattering of the People
    a. Genesis 10-11

CHAPTER 1: GOD BUILDS HIS NATION— Israel Chosen As The People Of Promise (c. 2000 – 931 BC)

GEN 12 – 1 KINGS 11

5. Patriarchs (2090 – 1875 BC)
    a. Genesis 11:27 – 50:26
    b. Job
6. Exodus (1875 – 1405 BC)
    a. Exodus (1875 – 1445 BC)
    b. Leviticus (1445 BC)

---

[2] Easley did not date this period; however, using the genealogical tables in Genesis 5, I believe the first 11 chapters of Genesis happened over an approximate 2000 year time period.

c. Numbers 1-13 (1445/44 BC)

7. Wanderings (1444 – 1405 BC)
    a. Numbers 14 – Deuteronomy 34 (1444 – 1405 BC)
8. Conquest of the Land (1405 – 1380 BC)
    a. Joshua (1405 – 1380 BC)
9. Judges (1380 – 1045 BC)
    a. Judges – 1 Samuel 7
    b. Ruth
10. United Kingdom (1045 – 931 BC)
    a. 1 Samuel 8 – 1 Kings 11
    b. 1 Chronicles – 2 Chronicles 9
    c. Psalms
    d. Proverbs
    e. Ecclesiastes
    f. Song of Solomon

CHAPTER 2: GOD EDUCATES HIS NATION— Disobedient Israel Disciplined (c. 931 – 586 BC)

1 KINGS 12 – 2 KINGS 25; SOME PROPHETS

11. Divided Kingdom (931 – 722 BC)
    a. 1 Kings 12 – 2 Kings 25
    b. 2 Chronicles 10-36
    c. Obadiah (840 BC)
    d. Joel (835 BC)
    e. Jonah (760 BC)
    f. Amos (755 BC)
    g. Hosea (755 – 710 BC)
    h. Isaiah (740 – 680 BC)

i. Micah (735 – 710 BC)

12. Judah Alone (722 – 605 BC)
    a. Nahum (663 – 612 BC)
    b. Zephaniah (630-625 BC)
    c. Jeremiah (627 – 580 BC)
    d. Habakkuk (607 BC)

CHAPTER 3: GOD KEEPS A FAITHFUL REMNANT—
Messiah's Space And Time Prepared (c. 586 – 6 BC)

EZRA THROUGH ESTHER; SOME PROPHETS

13. Babylonian Captivity (606 – 536 BC)
    a. Daniel (605 – 536 BC)
    b. Ezekiel (592 – 570 BC)
14. Return (536 – 425 BC)
    a. Ezra 1-6 (538 – 515 BC)
    b. Haggai (520 BC)
    c. Zechariah (520 – 470 BC)
    d. Esther (483 – 473 BC)
    e. Ezra 7-10 (457 BC)
    f. Nehemiah (444 – 425 BC)
    g. Malachi (432 – 425 BC)
15. Years of Silence (400 BC)
    a. Amos 8:11

CHAPTER 4: GOD PURCHASES REDEMPTION &
BEGINS THE KINGDOM—
Jesus The Messiah, 6 BC – 30 AD

THE GOSPELS

16. Life of Christ (33 AD)
    a. Matthew
    b. Mark
    c. Luke
    d. John

CHAPTER 5: GOD SPREADS THE KINGDOM THROUGH THE CHURCH—
The current age, 30 A.D. - ?

ACTS & THE EPISTLES

17. Early Church (33 – 100 AD)
    a. Acts – Jude
18. Current Age (100 AD to Present)

CHAPTER 6: GOD CONSUMMATES REDEMPTION & CONFIRMS HIS ETERNAL KINGDOM

REVELATION 1 – 20; OTHER SCRIPTURES

19. Return of Christ (?)
    a. Revelation 1-20

Epilogue: New Heaven & New Earth

REVELATION 21 – 22

20. Dwelling with God
    a. Revelation 21-22

Now that you have the big-picture summary of the Bible, at this point, I will elaborate on the summary (prologue, the chapters, the epilogue, and the 20 major events) to provide a detailed explanation for each of these topics.

PROLOGUE: NEED FOR REDEMPTION

GENESIS 1-11 – "God is building a kingdom of redeemed people because human beings are sinners and not holy enough to be with God. Human beings by their own merit cannot earn their way to dwell with the one true and living God. These 11 chapters show mankind has rebelled against God since the creation of man."[3]

The first 11 chapters of Genesis explain the need for redemption through four great events: creation; fall of man; flood; and the tower of Babel (scattering of the people).

Let's examine the major subsections of the prologue, and break them down, showing the appropriate books and chapters of the Bible that go along with them.

---

[3] Easley, 5.

Creation

Genesis 1-5

Question: Have you ever wondered why God created us?

Answer: If you pay careful attention to the one-sentence summary listed above, you will see two operative words: joy and glory. God created us for His glory and for our joy. A personal, close relationship with Him is the means. We learn God created us for His glory by reading Revelation 4:11,

> *"You are worthy, our Lord and God, to receive glory and honor and power, for you created all things, and by your will they were created and have their being."*

Colossians 1:16 and Ephesians 3:8-12 provide us with further rationale.

"Being made in the image and likeness of God (Genesis 1:27), human beings have the ability to know God and therefore love Him, worship Him, serve Him, and fellowship with Him. If we had never existed, God would still be God—the unchanging One (Malachi 3:6). The I AM (Exodus 3:14) was never dissatisfied with His own eternal existence. When He made the universe, He did what pleased Himself, and since God is perfect, His action was perfect. 'It was very good.'[1] (Genesis 1:31)

---

[1] Got Questions Ministries, 2018.

The Fall of Man

Genesis 3

Question: Have you ever wondered why Adam and Eve fell?

Answer: God created Adam and Eve and gave them freedom of choice. When they were tempted in the Garden of Eden, and they decided to eat of the tree of "the knowledge of good and evil" their eyes were "opened" and they realized they had broken God's law. As a result of their experience with sin, they no longer warranted a place in the presence of God, who is holy and without sin. Genesis chapter three tells us how God established man's life on this earth based on the sin that entered the world through Adam and Eve.

Flood

Genesis 6-9

Question: Why did God flood the earth?

Answer: In Genesis 1:31, when God had finished creating the heaven and the earth, He looked upon His creation, and "saw everything He had made, and behold, it was very good." But by the time we arrive at Genesis 6:15, "The LORD saw how great the wickedness of the human race had become on the earth, and that every inclination of the thoughts of the human heart was only evil all the time." There were only ten generations from Adam and Eve in the garden until the flood. By this time, only eight people were considered godly, and as a result, God determined (in his holiness and justness) the world should be destroyed with a flood.

Scattering of the People

Genesis 10-11

Question: Why did God get so angry and change their language?

Answer: The people were being disobedient. God commanded them to "Be fruitful and multiply, and fill the earth." (Genesis 9:7) However, they were settling, conspiring, being prideful, and not filling the earth. God knew they would turn to evil things by working collectively. We read in Genesis 11:6, "Behold, they are one people, and have one language, and this is only the beginning of what they will do. And nothing they propose to do will now be impossible for them." So God changed their language, and they were scattered.

The first 11 chapters of Genesis explain man's need for redemption before he can come into contact with the holy God.

CHAPTER 1: GOD BUILDS HIS NATION
Israel chosen as the people of promise, c. 2000 – 931 BC

GENESIS 12 – 1 KINGS 11 – "The first chapter in God's plan to build an everlasting kingdom was to build an earthly nation in a particular time and place.

This chapter carries the plot from the first family He called to His covenant (Abraham and Sarah) to the full splendor of the Israelite nation at its grandest expression (under David and Solomon)."[2]

After the scattering at the Tower of Babel, the next major event we read about is the Patriarchs.

Patriarchs
(2090 – 1875 BC)

Genesis 11:27 – 50:26

Job

Question: Who were the Patriarchs?

Answer: The biblical patriarchs were the lineage of men God used to establish Israel as a nation. God chose Abraham because of his faith, and made a covenant with him that he would be "the father of many nations." (Genesis 17:4).

Abraham's wife, Sarah, was in her nineties and she doubted she could bear children; however, she gave birth to Isaac (Genesis 21:2). Isaac was a man of great faith, who fathered Jacob(who was also given the name "Israel"). Jacob's sons became the patriarchs of the twelve tribes of Israel. The tribes were called: Reuben, Simeon, Levi, Judah, Zebulon, Issachar, Dan, Gad, Asher, Naphtali, Benjamin, and Joseph's sons Ephraim and Manasseh.[3]

---

[2] Easley, 6.

[3] Got Questions: Who were the Patriarchs?

Exodus
(1875 - 1405 BC)

Exodus (1875 – 1445 BC)
Leviticus (1445 BC)
Numbers 1-13 (1445/44 BC)

Question: What was the Exodus?

Answer: Jacob's son Joseph was sold into slavery by his brothers, but was the conduit through which God would save them by bringing them to Egypt where there was food. After he died, the Israelites were made slaves of the Egyptian pharaohs. The Israelites cried out to God for deliverance, and God sent Moses to lead them out of exile. We read of the story of the Exodus in the books of Exodus, Leviticus, Numbers and Deuteronomy.

Wanderings
(1444 - 1405 BC)

Numbers 14 – Deuteronomy 34 (1444 – 1405 BC)

Question: Why was Israel cursed with forty years of wilderness wandering?

Answer: As they approached the land of Canaan, the Israelites sent twelve spies out to assess the people who inhabited it. Ten of the spies were convinced they could not defeat the inhabitants, even though God assured them He would deliver their enemies to them. Those ten spies stirred up the dissent of the people;

however, two of the spies, Joshua and Caleb believed God, and they were the only two who entered the land.

As a result of the unbelief and disobedience of the people, God's wrath was stirred against them, and He cursed them with forty years (one year for each of the forty days they explored the land) wandering in the wilderness until the generation of unbelievers died. Not one of the unbelievers entered into the promised land of Canaan.

Conquest of the Land (1405 - 1380 BC)

Joshua (1405 – 1380 BC)

Question: What was the conquest of the land?

Answer: Joshua led the Israelite army to defeat the people of Jericho in chapter 6. Achan was disobedient in chapter 7, so there was a setback; but soon Ai was captured. Joshua defeats the armies of the southern part of Canaan in chapters 9–10 and all the northern part in chapter 11. In chapters 13–21, the land is divided to the tribes of Israel. God have given the Israelites their victories, and Joshua proclaimed before his death that the Israelites should remember to love (be obedient to) God if they wanted to prosper.

Judges (1380 - 1045 BC)

Judges, Ruth, 1 Samuel 1-7

Question: Who were the Judges?

Answer: After the conquest of the land, judges were established to lead the Israelites occasionally, as military leaders and to settle legal matters. Judges led the people during times of crisis until the formation of the first Kingdom of Israel (ca. 1150–1025 BC). The Book of Judges lists twelve leaders who judged Israel: Othniel, Ehud, Shamgar, Deborah, Gideon, Tola, Jain, Jephthah, Ibzan, Elon, Abdon, and Samson. Other judges are listed in First Samuel and First Chronicles as well as Second Chronicles.

United Kingdom
(1045 - 931 BC)

1 Samuel 8 – 1 Kings 11

1 Chronicles – 2 Chronicles 9

Psalms

Proverbs

Ecclesiastes

Song of Solomon

Question: What was the United Kingdom?

Answer: The United Kingdom consisted of the twelve tribes of Israel during the reigns of the first three kings: Saul, David, and Solomon. These kings reigned between 1045 and 931 BC. The Israelites were at the height of their earthly glory during this time. After Solomon's death, the Kingdom split into two kingdoms: the Kingdom of Israel (whose main cities were Shechem and Samaria) in the north and the Kingdom of Judah (whose capital was Jerusalem) in the south. The United Kingdom Timeline 1, listed below, shows some of the major events under the three kings of the United Kingdom.

United Kingdom Timeline[4]

1045-1011 BC
Saul reigns over the twelve tribes of Israel

1012 BC David kills the Philistine champion, Goliath of Gath.

1011 BC Saul is killed by the Philistines at the battle of Gilboa.

1011-1004 BC
David is king in Judah
Ishbosheth reigns over the rest of Israel

1011 BC Ishbosheth, Saul's son, becomes king of Israel

1011 BC David becomes king of Judah at Hebron.

1004 BC Ishbosheth is murdered, and David becomes king over all Israel and Judah.

1004-971 BC
David reigns over a reunited kingdom of Israel

1004 BC David conquers Jerusalem, and brings the

---

[4] This outline is based on one found at The Bible Journey Website. All dates are approximate.

	Ark of the Covenant there.
999 BC	David has an affair with Bathsheba, and has her husband murdered.
995 BC	David's son Absolom rises in revolt and claims the throne, forcing David to reign in exile at Manahaim..
984 BC	David defeats Absolom at the battle of Ephraim, and returns to Jerusalem to again reign over Israel.
982 BC	David purchases the land on which the Temple would later be built.
971 BC	David dies

971-931 BC
Solomon reigns as king of Israel

968 BC	Solomon begins to build the Temple in Jerusalem
961 BC	Solomon finishes building the Temple
948 BC	Solomon finishes building his palace in Jerusalem.
931 BC	Solomon dies, and his son, Rehoboam, becomes king over all Israel.
931 BC	Israel rebels against Rehoboam over taxes, dividing the kingdom once again.
931 BC	Jeroboam becomes king of Israel. Rehoboam reigns only over Judah.

Many of the **Psalms**, the Book of **Proverbs**, the **Song of Songs** and the Book of **Ecclesiastes** were written around this time

As the Israelites multiplied in number, they drifted farther and farther away from God, but God stayed with them because of the covenants He made with them and knowing in His time that all of His plans would be fulfilled.

CHAPTER 2: GOD EDUCATES HIS NATION Disobedient Israel disciplined c. 931 – 586 B.C.

1 KINGS 12 – 2 KINGS 25; SOME PROPHETS – "The second chapter in God's plan was to educate Israel about the consequences of sin. The Israelites compromised by worshipping other gods during the entire time they were in the land. God raised His spokesmen, the Prophets, to urge people to repent of idolatry and injustice, to warn of the coming "day of the LORD" in judgment. They also predicted the coming of the Messiah. Their message was largely ignored. This chapter carries the plot from the division of the nation (because of sin) to its destruction (because of sin)."[5]

---

[5] Easley, 6.

Divided Kingdom
(931 - 722 BC)

1 Kings 12 – 2 Kings 25
2 Chronicles 10-36
Obadiah (840 BC)
Joel (835 BC)
Jonah (760 BC)
Amos (755 BC)
Hosea (755 – 710 BC)
Isaiah (740 – 680 BC)
Micah (735 – 710 BC)

Question: What was the Divided Kingdom?

Answer: The apex for the Israelites' earthly kingdom came during the reigns of Kings David and Solomon. The United Kingdom began to fracture under David when his son, Absalom began to revolt and pull followers away from David. The kingdom fractured even further during Solomon's reign and split during the reign of his son, Rehoboam.

God divided the kingdom because the people forsook Him and did not walk in His ways. The Lord sent the prophet, Ahijah to inform Solomon's servant Jeroboam that God was going to give him authority over ten tribes of Israel.

After Solomon died, his son Rehoboam became king. Shortly thereafter, as Ahijah had prophesied, Jeroboam confronted Rehoboam and demanded lighter taxes for the people. Rehoboam refused to concede, so

Jeroboam and ten of the twelve tribes of Israel rejected Rehoboam's authority, and divided the kingdom.

Jeroboam became king over the ten northernmost tribes, which they continued to call "Israel." Rehoboam remained the king of the southern kingdom of Judah, which consisted of two tribes – Benjamin and Judah.

Disobedience to God—sin—divided the kingdom. (1 Corinthians 1:13; 11:18 and James 4:1).

The Divided Kingdom Timeline

The Divided Kingdom
931 – 722 BC

Kingdom of Judah		Kingdom of Israel	
931-914	Rehoboam	Jeroboam	**931-911**
914-913	Abijah		
912-871	Asa	Nadab	**911-910**
		Baasha	**910-887**
		Elah	**887-886**
		Zimri	**886**
		Tibni	**886-883**
		Omri	**883-874**
871-849	Jehoshaphat	Ahab	**874-852**
		Ahaziah	**852-851**
849-842	Jehoram	Joram/Jehoram	**851-842**
842	Ahaziah	Jehu	**842-813**
842-836	Queen Athaliah		
836-796	Joash	Jehoahaz	**813-797**
796-768	Amaziah	Jehoash	**797-783**
768-738	Azariah/Uzziah	Jeroboam II[6]	**793-751**
747-736	Jotham[7]	Zechariah	**751**
		Shallum	**751**
		Menahem	**751-741**

---

[6] Jeroboam II reigned as co-regent with his father for a decade.

[7] Jotham became co-regent around a decade before his father's death.

		Pekahiah	**741-740**
		Pekah	**740-732**
736-728	Ahaz	Hoshea	**732-722**
728-695	Hezekiah	**CONQUERED**	**722**

Significant Events

931 Jeroboam introduces false worship, in an effort to keep the northern citizens from going to Jerusalem to worship.

910 Baasha kills Nadab and takes the throne, ending Jeroboam's family line.

886 Zimri murders Elah, ending Baasha's family line, and takes the throne. He in turn commits suicide seven days later when the army comes after him.

886 Tibni and Omri are both declared king by different factions, but Omri quickly disposes of Tibni and takes the throne.

881 Capitol moved to Samaria

874 Ahab inherits the throne on the death of his father. He marries Jezebel, a Gentile pagan, who in turn murders many faithful followers of God.

870-867 Massive drought foretold by Elijah, which led to his showdown on Mt. Carmel with the prophets of Baal.

852 Ahab is killed in battle.

842 Jehu accepts his divine mission to kill King Joram/Jehoram (of Israel), also kills King Jehoram (of Judah) before going to Samaria and having Jezebel killed.

842 Athaliah (daughter of Ahab and Jezebel, and mother-in-law of Jehoram of Judah) murders all the royal seed, but misses the baby that was taken to safety.

840 Obadiah prophesies against Edom for taking advantage of Judah after an invasion.

836 7-year old Joash, surrounded by soldiers under orders from the priest, is revealed to be alive, and is proclaimed king as Athaliah is killed outside the Temple.

751 King Zechariah is murdered by Shallum, ending Jehu's royal line. Shallum reigned one month before himself being murdered.

760-725 Amos, Hosea, Micah, and Isaiah prophesy against the wickedness of Israel. Jonah prophesies against Nineveh.

733 Tiglath-Pileaser, king of Assyria, captures Galilee and deports the citizens to Assyria.

724-722 Shalmaneser V (king of Assyria) lays siege to Samaria, and finally takes all of the northern kingdom as hostages to be exiled in Assyria.

Judah Alone (722 - 605 BC)

Nahum (663 – 612 BC)
Zephaniah (630-625 BC)
Jeremiah (627 – 580 BC)
Habakkuk (607 BC)

"The southern kingdom of Judah – with its capital at Jerusalem - lasted a further 135 years before the Babylonian conquest in 587 BC. The exiles began returning from Babylon fifty years later in 537 BC, but the restored walls of Jerusalem were not completed until 445BC."[8]

The Kingdom of Judah Timeline[9]

728-695	Hezekiah
695-641	Manassah
641-639	Amon
639-608	Josiah
608	Jehoahaz
608-598	Jehoiakim
598	Jehoiachin
597-586	Zedekiah

Significant Events

710 Hezekiah shows Babylonian envoys the treasures of Judah without giving the glory to God, and is told that Babylon will eventually conquer Judah.

695 Manasseh takes the throne and plunges Judah into idolatry, including sacrificing his own son to a false god.[10]

---

[8] The Bible Journey Website: Judah Alone

[9] Ibid

c. 647 Manasseh is captured by Assyria, and while a prisoner in chains, he repents of his wickedness. When he returns to Judah, he tries to undo all his wickedness, and partially succeeds.

627 Jeremiah begins his prophetic ministry, calling the people to repentance, and warning about destruction. Zephaniah also prophesies of judgment for disobedience.

623 The book of the law (of Moses) is found, leading king Josiah to institute a massive restoration movement, and directing the people back to God.

615 Nahum foretells the imminent destruction of Assyria by Babylon, which took place around 3 years later.

608 Josiah is killed in battle with the king of Egypt.

608 The king of Egypt removes Josiah's son, Jehoahaz, from the throne, and replaces him with Jehoiakim.

607 Habakkuk asks God to act in judgment against Israel for their wickedness, and God tells him that judgment is about to come in the form of the Babylonian armies.

605 Nebuchadnezzar invades Judah and sub-

---

[10] Jewish tradition says Manasseh later murdered the prophet Isaiah.

jugates it. He takes many of the royal family as hostages (including Daniel).

602 Jehoiakim rebels against Nebuchadnezzar.

598 Nebuchadnezzar returns and besieges Jerusalem, taking even more citizens (including Ezekiel) captive to Babylon.

589 Ezekiel prophesies the destruction of Jerusalem.

589 Zedekiah, king of Judah, rebels, causing another siege of Jerusalem.

587-586 The population of Jerusalem and Judah are exiled to Babylon, and the Temple and palace are completely destroyed.

586 Jeremiah, who escaped to Egypt, writes the book of Lamentations, bewailing what happened to Jerusalem and the citizens because of their sin.

CHAPTER 3: GOD KEEPS A FAITHFUL REMNANT Messiah's space and time prepared 586 – 6 B.C.

EZRA THROUGH ESTHER; SOME PROPHETS – "Chapter three in God's story is the "quiet chapter." Outwardly, it appeared that God was doing nothing for more than five centuries. For those who read the story carefully, however, He was doing two important things. On one hand, God was keeping the Jews together as a nation. They had their own land, laws, and temple, even though the kingship and national independence had disappeared. God was preparing to send His son in the fullness of time. On the other hand, God scattered most Jews throughout the nations to be testimonies to His name. This chapter carries the plot from the Babylonian captivity until the birth of the Messiah."[11]

Babylonian Captivity (606 - 536 BC)

Daniel (605 – 536 BC)
Ezekiel (592 – 570 BC)

Question: What was the Babylonian captivity?

Answer: The Babylonian captivity was a time period when the Israelites were subjects of Babylon, starting under king Nebuchadnezzar II.

The Israelites from the southern kingdom of Judah were taken captive because of their idolatry and disobedience. The Israelites were captives between 606 and 536 BC, and as prophesied by Jeremiah and Isaiah, after 70 years, King Cyrus of Persia allowed the Israelites to return to Jerusalem to begin rebuilding the city and temple. This 70-year captivity resulted in a renewed obedience to God, and for the first time in the history of the Israelite people, they stopped worshipping idols.

---

[11] Easley, 6.

Return
(536 - 425 BC)

Ezra 1-6 (538 – 515 BC)
Haggai (520 BC)
Zechariah (520 – 470 BC)
Esther (483 – 473 BC)
Ezra 7-10 (457 BC)
Nehemiah (444 – 425 BC)
Malachi (432 – 425 BC)

Question: What was the Return (to Zion)?

Answer: The Israelites' return to Jerusalem (Zion) happened approximately 536 B.C. God spoke through the prophets to inform the people they would return from captivity after 70 years.

The Persian ruler, Cyrus conquered the Babylonians and granted a decree for them to return to Jerusalem. Because there were tens of thousands of Israelites in Babylon, they exited in four waves known as *Aliyah.*

Approximately 50,000 Israelites returned to Jerusalem in Sheshbazzar's Aliyah, Zerubbabel's Aliyah, Ezra's Aliyah, and Nehemiah's Aliyah.

Years of Silence
(400 BC)

Amos 8:11

Question: What were the years of silence?

Answer: The 400 years of silence was a time period between the Old Testament and New Testament when

God did not speak to the Israelites through prophets. Although God did not speak to the people, He was preparing the way for the Messiah to come.

The Greeks and Romans ruled during this period and made significant contributions to the civilized world. Greek became the "universal" language for educated people in the region,and the Romans developed intricate roadways which allowed travel times to be severely diminished. Both language and roads were critical to the spreading of the gospel when Jesus commissioned His disciples.

CHAPTER 4: GOD PURCHASES REDEMPTION & BEGINS THE KINGDOM

Jesus the Messiah

6 B.C. – 30 A.D.

THE GOSPELS – "The fourth chapter in God's plan to build an everlasting kingdom of redeemed people is the most important one of all – the four Gospels. It shows how God's unconditional covenant promises – first to Abraham, then to David – were fulfilled by the new covenant of Jesus. This chapter carries the plot from the birth of the Messiah to His resurrection and exaltation."[12]

---

[12] Easley, 6.

Life of Christ
(6 BC - 30 AD)

Matthew
Mark
Luke
John

The Life of Christ: The gospel books of Matthew, Mark, Luke, and John give us a first-hand account of Jesus's life on this earth. When one considers that Jesus was in heaven with God the Father, and He willingly came to earth to be like us (in bodily form) so we would have a chance to be like Him (in spiritual form), it is incomprehensible.

Jesus not only sacrificed Himself, He bore the sins of mankind to allow man to dwell with a holy God for eternity. Think on these things!

CHAPTER 5:
GOD SPREADS THE KINGDOM THROUGH THE CHURCH

"ACTS & THE EPISTLES – With Chapter five in God's story, we come to our own part of the story. We belong here. This is the period of the Great Commission, when God's plan no longer focuses on persons of one ethnic group in one place (Israel). He is now redeeming persons out of every ethnic group in every place. Wherever and whenever God's people are, they meet as churches, worshiping communities of the new covenant. From Pentecost until the end-time scenario unfolds, God is about the business of spreading the message of the kingdom through the church."[13]

Early Church
(33 - 100 AD)

Acts – Jude

Question: What is significant about the early church?

Answer: The New Testament pattern of the early Christian church began at the day of Pentecost, which you can read about in Acts 2:1-3. During a supper gathering of the disciples, they witnessed the coming of the Holy Spirit (which Jesus had foretold) to dwell in believers. The Holy Spirit gave "gifts" to Jesus's disciples, such as the ability to speak in tongues (different languages), the ability to perform miracles, the ability to cast out demons, the ability to raise people from the dead, to prophesy, as well as other gifts. The intent of these gifts was to spread the name of Jesus, so people may believe He was the Son of God. In believing, people would be baptized in the name of the Father, the Son, and the Holy Spirit for the remission of sins and be added to the spiritual kingdom of Christ. The apostles who possessed the gifts of the Holy Spirit could impart these gifts to those on whom they laid hands. When the people who had received these gifts

---

[13] Ibid.

from the apostles died, these gifts of the Holy Spirit ceased to exist.

The reason they ceased to exist was because they had served God's purposes – to begin and grow members who were added to the church of Christ (that is the church that belongs to Jesus).

Some believe people still possess these gifts of the Holy Spirit that were given on the day of Pentecost – ***do not allow the devil to deceive you*** – this is false doctrine. If someone is adamant they have gifts, please have them show you how they can raise someone from the dead – it will never happen, so they do not possess the gifts of the Holy Spirit that were given to the apostles.

The Current Age
(100 AD - Present)

Question: What is significant about the current age?

Answer: The early church or spiritual kingdom spread rapidly for the first one hundred years, even though Christians suffered many persecutions from the Roman Emperors. In this current age, Christians continue to have the responsibility to spread the name of Jesus so people may believe and be baptized (a complete water submersion, not a sprinkling of water) for the remission of sins.

We must be mindful of our purpose on this earth; otherwise, one will not experience the joy God intended for man to have while in bodily form and even more so in spiritual form when Jesus returns to judge all who have ever lived.

CHAPTER 6:
GOD DELIVERS & CONFIRMS HIS ETERNAL KINGDOM

REVELATION 1–20; OTHER SCRIPTURES – "In Chapter six, God's plan to build an everlasting kingdom of redeemed people through His Christ for their joy and for His own glory is fully realized. Students often disagree about how Revelation is interpreted but main points are clear."[14] Regardless of persecution, trials, or even death, those who stay true to Christ will be victorious and share in His glory.[15]

The Return of Christ

Question: What is significant about the return of Christ?

Answer: Only God the Father knows the time when Jesus will return. Neither the angels nor the Son know when that hour will be (Matthew 24:36). John tells us that Jesus voluntarily submitted to have His omniscience restricted to be obedient to the Father. (John 15:15) Obedience is important to God, and He desires mankind to submit to His will just as Jesus did. Although Jesus has been restricted in knowing the hour of His return, the Father has given Him all authority to judge mankind.

When Jesus returns every knee shall bow and every tongue shall confess He is Lord. (Romans 14:11) It will be a time when every person who has ever lived will be judged (2 Corinthians 5:10; Acts 17:30-31). There is a simple formula to ensure you are ready for Jesus's return.

---

[14] Easley, 7.

[15] Differing views include (1) that it is speaking of the ultimate downfall of Rome—the persecutor of Christians, (2) that it is speaking of the destruction of Jerusalem—the Jews being the biggest persecutor of Christians in Acts, (3) that it is speaking of the final judgment at the end of the world, and (4) a combination of any of the three previous choices. This isn't a complete list, but it is representative of most of the views held by members of the church.

Hear – Believe – Repent – Confess – Be Baptized – Live Faithfully (Obedience)

Hear:

*"So then faith comes by **hearing**, and **hearing** by the Word of God." (Romans 10:17)*

Believe:

*"Whoever **believes** and is baptized will be saved, but whoever does not believe will be condemned." (Mark 16:16)*

Repent:

*"I tell you, no, but unless you **repent**, you will all likewise perish." (Luke 13:3)*

Confess:

*"And I say to you, everyone who **confesses** Me before men, the Son of Man will **confess** him also before the angels of God." (Luke 12:8)*

Be Baptized[16]:

*"Whoever believes and is **baptized** will be saved, but whoever does not believe will be condemned." (Mark 16:16)*

---

[16] "If belief is a condition to be saved, then Baptism must be a condition to be saved since they are joined by the conjunction 'and.' Faith and Baptism are of equal rank. If one is a condition of salvation, so is the other. If one is not a condition of pardon, neither is the other." (Larry Hafley – Guardian of Truth)

Live Faithfully (Obedience):

Jesus said, "If you love Me, you will keep My commandments." (John 14:15)

God expects us to be obedient to Him in our daily lives. We proved our love for God by our obedience. (1 John 5:2-3) Obedience or living faithfully gives us assurance that we "know" God and are worshipping Him in spirit and in truth. (1 John 2:3) Obedience to God is the least we can do because God has assured us we will dwell with Him for eternity if we worship as He pleases and live faithfully all the days of our lives.

EPILOGUE: NEW HEAVEN & NEW EARTH

REVELATION 21 – 22 – There will be no end to the kingdom of God. In their eternal state, the citizens of that kingdom will be filled with joy. There will be no more sin, no death, no temptation, and no separation from the Father who delivered them. Revelation 21 and 22 has been seen by many as a description of this post-judgment reality.[17] "The end of the story in time is only the beginning of the story in eternity, for *the Lord God through His Christ has graciously built a*

---

[17] Others hold that it is a reference to the spiritual blessings of the church on earth since the first century. Regardless of the interpretation of this passage, the Bible teaches the faithful will be with God after judgment (Matthew 25).

kingdom of redeemed people for their joy and for His own glory."[18]

Dwelling with God

"One thing I ask from the LORD, this only do I seek; that I may dwell in the house of the LORD all the days of my life, to gaze on the beauty of the LORD and to seek Him in His temple." (Psalm 27:4)

One of the most beautiful thoughts written by a man was the verse above written by David. This is one of my favorite verses, and I hid it in my heart long ago (Psalm 119:11). I often ponder or meditate on the relationship David had with God, and how I could have a closer, more intimate relationship with God. After all David had been through on this earth; after all his joys of dancing before the LORD and his lowest points of sinning against God, David managed to have the relationship with God that would allow this verse to flow from his pure heart.

David wrote there was one thing he desired of God: to dwell in His house so he could gaze upon God's beauty and to seek Him in His temple. Do you feel that way about God? Do you long to see His face to gaze upon His beauty? Do you long to seek Him in His temple? I pray you diligently seek a relationship with

---

[18] Ibid.

God where you long to dwell with Him and behold His glorious beauty!

6
Understanding the Importance of Spending Time Alone with God

"They went to a place called Gethsemane, and Jesus said to His disciples, 'sit here while I pray.' He took Peter, James, and John along with Him, and He began to be deeply distressed and troubled. 'My soul is overwhelmed with sorrow to the point of death,' He said to them. 'Stay here and keep watch.'"
(Mark 14:32-34)

Every relationship that brings joy must be cultivated. Most often, we get out of relationships what we put into them. Our relationship with God is no different. In order for us to experience the relationship with God that He intended—one that glorifies Him and brings us more joy than anything in this world—we must spend time alone with Him. This takes discipline, but most people are not very disciplined in their relationship with God. Most people do not pray or read and meditate on God's Word on a daily basis. And even more people do not experience the joy of being "ever conscious of God's presence" on a daily basis. For some Christians, these things come as they mature in their relationship with God; but for those who diligently seek God, this relationship comes sooner than later.

There is no secret or shortcut to developing a close relationship with God; it takes discipline. However, there are times when it will become more important to you than anything else because you hunger and thirst for the joy that only God may provide.

Jesus Withdrew

We see many examples of Jesus withdrawing from the people to be alone with God. Jesus took the time to focus on God the Father. He spent much time communicating to the Father in prayer and thought. What does His example tell us about how we should live our lives? We need to remember Jesus when we struggle for the discipline to spend time alone with God.

Daniel Prayed

Daniel was such a staunch child of God. Daniel had such a close relationship with God that we do not read about any of his shortcomings. I believe this was because Daniel spent time alone with God in prayer on a daily basis, and that kept him focused on God.

Some months ago, I had about a six-month period where I had more trials and tribulations than I had previously had in all my life combined. Yes, I had more burdens than ever, and every single one of them was out of my control. There was nothing I could do to eliminate any of these major obstacles. I was in deep despair. My spirit was distressed like I have never experienced in my life. I was as low as perhaps I had been on this earth.

I subscribe to a daily devotional where I receive two emails each morning with thoughts about God and verses to meditate upon each day. On this morning of deep despair, I suddenly awoke around 4:00 a.m., and I began crying and praying that God would relieve me from the despair of my heart. Then I opened my daily thought emails about God. The thought on that morning was about Daniel spending time alone with God in prayer.

In Daniel 6, we read about the administrators and satraps of King Darius who were jealous of Daniel. They knew the only way they could devise a scheme against him was to accuse him of something that would come between him and God, because Daniel was a righteous man who feared the LORD. So they deviously asked the king to sign a decree that would prohibit anyone from bowing to any God or anyone other than the king—or they would be put to death. In verse 10, we see how Daniel responded to this decree.

When Daniel knew the decree had been signed, he went home to his upper room, faced toward Jerusalem, and knelt on his knees three times that day to give thanks to God, as was his custom since his youth.

In the early morning hours on that day of my deep despair, this verse lifted my burden tremendously. I felt God had used the author to send that verse to me on that day. Let me explain why.

First, notice in verse 10 what Daniel did not pray for. He did not pray that God would save his life from the lions. He did not appear to even mention that he had any concern whatsoever that his life may have ended soon. No, Daniel was not worried about the king's decrees. He was not worried about dying as a young man.

Second, and the amazing thing, is not only was Daniel not worried about dying or being falsely accused, he gave *thanks* to God three times that day as he had always done since his youth. Daniel was obedient to God; he was righteous before the Lord. He had a close relationship with God that comforted him in times of what would have been deep despair for many people. He trusted God.

My burden was lifted, as I meditated on that verse. I did not fear that I would be put to death, so all of my burdens – though more than I had experienced in my life combined – would not result in the loss of my life. That was a lesson to me. It made me want to have the relationship with God that Daniel displayed. So, how did Daniel develop this relationship with God?

Daniel had an intimate relationship with God, at least in part, because of the time alone he spent with God in prayer … on his knees. The world has polluted our thoughts of God, and we look to others around us to base our spiritual lives upon. Do not practice looking at others to achieve your spiritual standard. This is ineffective.

God wants us to spend time alone with Him in prayer like Jesus did and like Daniel did. That means we must do much more than the few minutes of prayer we give to God each day. Prayers while we are driving do not allow us to focus on a holy God. We must discipline ourselves to get on our knees in prayer at least two or three times per day. We need to set regular time aside to dedicate time alone with God – not only in prayer, but also in Bible study, meditating on God's ways, singing joyfully to God and worshipping Him.

If you make a commitment to set time aside to kneel in prayer, you will begin to see your relationship with God draw closer in a short period of time. Perhaps if your life is ever threatened because you are obedient to God, instead of panicking for your life to be spared, maybe you will be like Daniel and thank God, knowing He will take care of you because of the faith you have developed in your close relationship with Him – all because you took the time to kneel in prayer and be alone with God on a daily basis.

7
Understanding the Importance of Worshipping God in Spirit and Truth

---

"God is Spirit and they who worship Him must worship in Spirit and Truth."
(John 4:24)

Definition of Worshipping in Truth

My definition of worshipping God in truth is to worship God by the pattern laid out in the New Testament. This is important because we know the early Christians were in an "approved" relationship with God according to Ephesians 1:7.

Definition of Worshipping in Spirit.

My definition of worshipping God in spirit is being ever conscious of God's presence, and viewing life with Him as center. This causes us to worship with a humble, loving attitude toward our Creator.

Doctrine versus Spirituality

Now that we have defined what it means to worship God in Spirit and in Truth, it is necessary to distinguish between (1) worshipping God by focusing on church doctrine versus (2) worshipping God spiritually or from within one's spirit.

Doctrine

I love my brothers and sisters who are members of local churches of Christ around the world, but their staunch focus on doctrinal beliefs, without cultivating a deep, abiding relationship with God, has destroyed many good men and split many local congregations. The church in Ephesus was warned by Jesus Himself that their purity of doctrine wasn't going to save them, because they lacked love (Revelation 2). The focus on external actions has destroyed the potential for growth in those local bodies of the church. They boast about "rightly dividing" the Word of Truth, and often with an ungentle and uncompassionate attitude toward their brethren, they split the church and cause faithful Christians to fall away. In many of these instances, those who "fell away" had good hearts. Pray if you are in the middle of this situation or have experienced it.

I'm not talking about having to stand up against wolves in sheep's clothing, who are trying to gain power or introduce damnable heresies. The point I am making is that some Christians believe "true worship" to God is following a checklist of specific actions done in specific ways—without any reference to the heart behind it. For example, *I sing songs, take the Lord's Supper, listen to a man preach a sermon, put money in the plate, hear a man pray, therefore based on doing those things, I am right with God.* There is no checklist. And this attitude is immature before God.

This problem has been going on for decades. I mentioned previously about some of the writings of A.

W. Tozer. This is what he wrote before his death in 1963.

> *"Sound Bible exposition is an imperative must in the church of the Living God. Without it no church can be a New Testament church in any strict meaning of that term. But exposition may be carried on in such a way as to leave the hearers devoid of any true spiritual nourishment whatever. For it is not mere words that nourish the soul, but God Himself, and unless and until the hearers find God in* personal *(emphasis mine) experience they are not the better for having heard the truth."*[1]

God wants us to keep our eyes on Him! He wants us to follow the New Testament pattern of worship, make it our foundation of worship in the assembly and get on to the meat of the Word while chasing after God. The Bible is our medium to learn more about Him. This will help us move on to the personal or spiritual relationship with God that He desires.

Let me provide you with a clear example of doctrine versus spirituality, and how it split churches. There was a deep fraction among the people about whether or not churches could contribute money collected on the first day of the week (as we see from the example in 1 Corinthians 16:2) to help widows and orphans in their need.

---

[1] Tozer, The Pursuit of God, 217.

We do not see any New Testament pattern where Christian churches provided money to help orphans and widows except in 1 Timothy 5 and Acts 6; however, the widows supported in those two verses were members of those local churches. Otherwise, there would have been no scriptural authority for the churches to support them. However, if we have pursued God, we know He has an affinity for orphans and widows. James tells us in chapter 1 verse 27: "Pure and undefiled religion in the sight of our God and Father is this: to visit orphans and widows in their distress, and to keep oneself unstained by the world."

So how do we rectify the two? Well, we know money is collected on the first day of the week to bring people to a knowledge of Jesus and to help needy saints (God's people). If widows and orphans worship in that local congregation and they need financial assistance to survive, then the congregation has a God-given responsibility to help them.

What if the orphans and widows are not members of that local church? Is the church obligated to help them financially? The answer is that the local church has no authority to help from the funds collected to do God's work of spreading the message of Jesus and helping needy saints; however, it is the responsibility of all Christians to help those in need as they have the ability. In this case, individual Christians should seek to help visit orphans and widows – if they are concerned about practicing "pure and undefiled" religion before God.

Now here is the sad part: this has split many churches because some members were so tied up in making sure their doctrine was right that they ended up not helping anyone at all! In short, spiritual people look for a way to help those in need, while legalistic people look for reasons why they can't.

God is not happy with Christians and churches who blatantly miss the point of true service to Him. This brings tears to my eyes as I write this. It hurts me that God is not pleased, and it hurts me that people are missing "true worship" and a close relationship with the Almighty. Open their eyes, Lord!

This difference in worshipping God in doctrine only as opposed to doctrinally, in spirit and in truth, is seen when Jesus condemned some of the seven churches of Asia.

"To the angel of the church in Sardis write: These are the words of him who holds the seven spirits of God and the seven stars. I know your deeds; you have a reputation of being alive, but you are dead. Wake up! Strengthen what remains and is about to die, for I have found your deeds unfinished in the sight of my God. Remember, therefore, what you have received and heard; hold it fast, and repent. But if you do not wake up, I will come like a thief, and you will not know at what time I will come to you. Yet you have a few people in Sardis who have not soiled their clothes. They will

walk with me, dressed in white, for they are worthy. The one who is victorious will, like them, be dressed in white. I will never blot out the name of that person from the book of life, but will acknowledge that name before my Father and his angels."
(Revelation 3:1-5)

Jesus told them to wake up! The members of the church at Sardis were following doctrine, but spiritually they were dead. And because they were dead spiritually – asleep in the light – Jesus was not pleased with them.

There are many churches today who follow doctrine as closely as any man could, but they do not possess the Holy Spirit. They do not pursue God. They do not know "true worship," and they will not be approved by Jesus when He returns, because they sought Jesus with their lips, but their hearts were far from Him. My soul aches for people to come to an understanding of true worship so they can enjoy the relationship with God that He desires and He intended for His people, so they can give Him the glory He deserves.

I am also reminded about Jesus's rejection of those without pure hearts, who focused on serving Jesus doctrinally but not spiritually.

"Not everyone that says to me, LORD, LORD, shall enter into the kingdom of heaven; but he that does the will of my Father which is in heaven. Many will say to

me in that day, LORD, LORD, have we not prophesied in your name? and in your name cast out demons? and in your name done many wonderful works? And then will I profess to them, I never knew you: depart from me, you that work iniquity.
(Matthew 7:21-23)

I am so glad you are reading this right now. Please continue on your journey to find true worship in doctrine and spiritually. The kind of worship Jehovah expects from His people.

Please pray with me.

> *Our Father, God, in heaven. Lord, holy and reverend is Your name. Lord, we come humbly before You at this time, praying Lord, that You would open the eyes of so many people in the world who focus so much on doctrine but have no knowledge of what You expect in true worship in order to have the relationship with You that was intended to bring overwhelming joy, humility, and peace as we enter Your presence in prayer and in worship. Lord, God Almighty, please open the eyes of those who are asleep in Your light. We pray for their hearts. We pray they would engage to seek You more diligently and first – above all else – in this world. The glory belongs to You. In the Holy name of Jesus we pray, amen.*

Spirituality

David Danced Before the Lord (2 Samuel 6:1-19)

As I previously provided an example of doctrine versus spirituality regarding the assistance of orphans and widows, now let me provide an example of spirituality, which is far from any doctrine but still pleasing to God.

In the book of Second Samuel, we read about David and the Ark of God. God's Holy Spirit dwelt enthroned above the cherubs on the Ark's cover (1 Samuel 4:4 and Psalm 80:1). In verse 12, David moved the Ark up to Jerusalem. He worshipped God with offerings, and verse 14 tells us David was so jubilant, so joyful that "he danced before the Lord with all his might." Can you imagine that? Have you ever had so much excitement, happiness, and joy in God that you felt like dancing in praise to him?

Have you ever thought about the reactions of fans when their team wins the big game. Do they scream, jump, hug, etc? Those are things that came from within, expressions of excitement, happiness, and joy. No one commanded them to do it. They weren't doing it because they felt that there was some mandate or checklist they had to go through to express pleasure in their team's victory. In the same way, there are many different expressions of excitement and joy that a Christian can engage in outside of the worship assembly, and God approves them (obviously so long as they aren't violating any other command).

David was so moved by God's presence and His blessings in what the Ark symbolized that he could not help express himself in that manner. This is an example of possessing a spirit for God. Spirituality is necessary to worship God in spirit. It is mandated by God. This attitude must be present whether we are worshipping as an individual or in the assembly of the church.

Now, I'm not suggesting that we dance during the worship assembly. It would distract the worship of others and would be contrary to worshipping in a proper and orderly manner according to 1 Corinthians 14:40. My point is to show you how joyous David was about God. This is quite the contrast to many of our worship assemblies, where everyone looks dour, sour, and depressed!

If you do not have extreme joy and extreme sorrow at times (such as when partaking of the Lord's Supper) in your worship assembly, then perhaps you should verify it is according to the New Testament pattern of worship. If you know your church worship is doctrinally sound, is it spiritually sound? If you cannot feel God's presence, and your worship is not spiritual, continue exploring this book and most importantly, explore the Bible to get closer to true worship and to God.

How do we move to spirituality or true worship, both as an individual and in the church assembly?

Chase hard after God! Pursue God diligently! Seek to truly understand God's nature and attributes.

8
Understanding the Importance of Attitude (Preparing One's Mind)

"Hear, O Israel:
The LORD our God, the LORD is one.
Love the LORD your God with all your
heart and with all your soul
and with all your strength."
(Deuteronomy 6:5)

"But seek first the kingdom of God and His
righteousness and all these things
will be added to you."
(Matthew 6:33)

God expects us to commit ourselves to Him with our whole being. And in order for us to find the joy in our relationship with God that He intended, we will have to follow His words. Otherwise, we will be lacking and frustrated. "Much of the inner turmoil we experience comes from our never having fully made up our minds what to do about God."[1] That inner turmoil can disappear if you come to develop the ***joy*** in your

[1] Henry, Diligently Seeking God.

relationship with God by following this roadmap and developing a proper attitude.

Committing yourself wholly is not easy to do for some, especially for those who are newly baptized into Christ. It does get easier as the days go by if we develop the right attitude of reverence and humility toward God.

Once you begin to understand more about God and grow in your relationship with Him, you will realize the path of service to God is a roller coaster of successes and failures. This is understandable considering our frail frames and our human nature; however, we should always work to commit ourselves completely, display the proper attitude of reverence, and remain humble before the LORD.

Consider the attitude of the Israelites in Nehemiah 8:1-8. This is an example of commitment, reverence, and humility for God's Word. In these verses, Israelites of Judah had just returned from Babylonian Captivity. After being refined by being in captivity for 70 years, the Israelites began to display the proper attitude of reverence and humility before God. They asked Ezra the scribe to read God's law to them. As Ezra opened the Book of the Law, the people stood up from daybreak to the middle of the day, they praised God for His Word and fell on their faces in worship. This humble commitment to God and reverence for Him and His Holy Word is the proper attitude one should have when worshipping God.

In Revelation chapter two, we see the *improper* attitude of the church at Ephesus displayed in verse four: "Yet I hold this against you: You have forsaken the love you had at first." The Christians at Ephesus had failed to put God first; they had lost their reverence and humility before God. And God was not pleased. On the other hand, we have the example of the church at Macedonia in 2 Corinthians 8:2-5. Because the Christians there had the proper attitude toward God, they had overflowing joy. They considered it a privilege to share in service to the Lord's people. Verse five says they committed themselves first of all to the LORD. This is the proper attitude that God expects from His people. And until we commit ourselves fully to Him, we won't experience the joy God desires for us to have—which may only be obtained by having a proper attitude.

9
Understanding the New Testament Pattern of Worship

"Make every effort to keep the unity of the Spirit through the bond of peace. There is one body and one Spirit, just as you were called to one hope when you were called; one Lord, one faith, one baptism; one God and Father of all, who is over all and through all and in all."
(Ephesians 4:3-6)

The church of Christ was established in the first century. Christ's mission on Earth was to die for the sins of man, giving His blood for this purpose (John 3:16; Matthew 20:28). He sent forth His word, which tells the news of these blessings (Mark 16:15). Those who obeyed His word were made "free from sin" and were known as a "Church" in their respective localities (Romans 6:17-18; 16:16). The Holy Christian Bible shows what one must do to be made "free from sin" (Romans 10:9-10; Acts 2:38-42). The Christians' aim should be to follow this original pattern set forth in the New Testament.

The various local Churches established in the first century were not different denominations. This is evident from the fact that they were all based on the same teaching (1 Corinthians 4:17). Rather, they were each a local manifestation of the Church about which Jesus spoke in Matthew 16:18. The largest organization of which we can read in the New Testament is a local Church, and the largest office we can read of in the Bible is the elders (bishops) of a local Church (Philippians 1:1; Acts 14:23). They were not dependent upon synods, conventions, or ecclesiastical bodies for their direction. Rather, each Church was independently responsible to follow the teaching of Christ (Acts 20:32; 2 John 9-11).

Their worship was something in which all the Christians participated. On the first day of the week, they ate the Lord's Supper and gave as they had been prospered (Acts 20:7; 1 Corinthians 11:23-26; 16:1-2). Through their examples we learn how the Lord wants a Church to use its collected funds (Acts 4:34-35; 11:27-30; Philippians 4:15-16). Further acts of worship in which they participated were congregational singing, praying, and the preaching/hearing of God's word (Ephesians 5:19; 1 Timothy 2:8; Acts 20:7).

Today, some might wonder why it is important to be like the first Christians. First, all Bible believers agree that the early Christians were in a saved relationship with God (Ephesians 1:7). Second, apostasies were predicted (Acts 20:28-31; 1 Timothy 4:1-3). False teaching renders worship vain and is destructive to one's soul (Matthew 15:9; 2 John 9). Third, it was the intention of the Lord that His Church not pass away. It represents a relationship God planned from and for eternity (Ephesians 3:10-11). The various denominational names of our day and age were unknown in the first century.[1]

Without worshipping God in truth, it is impossible to be pleasing to Him, and we see myriad examples in the Old Testament where the people worshipped God in vain. They worshipped God in vain because they did not heed the pattern and instructions He gave them. This is true today when people do not worship God according to this New Testament pattern.

> *"The kind of Christianity prominent today does not know where it is and is trying to run a heavenly institution after an earthly manner. Now if this church is to be a church of Christ, a living organic member of that redeemed body of which Christ is Head, then its teachers and its members must strive earnestly and sacrificially and with constant prayer do a number of things. We must strive to make our practices New Testament in their content."*[2]

Now that you have Bible scriptures which point to worshipping God in truth, you must begin this pattern in the assembly to be pleasing to God, but do not forget what you learned from the section on doctrine versus spirituality. Worship to God is more than a check-

---

[1] Compiled by Mr. Steve Wallace, a former evangelist at the Ramstein, Germany church of Christ

[2] Tozer: Mystery of the Holy Spirit, 148.

list of doctrinal items, it must be done in spirit, as well as truth, to reach the throne of God and be pleasing to Him.

10
Understanding the Importance of Living an Obedient Life

Once Saved Always Saved?

Some maintain after one is baptized into Christ for the remission of sins, they can continue sinning because God is full of grace. They believe we sin no matter how hard we try, and because Jesus died for our sins, we can live any way we want, and still be with a holy God someday. Some go as far to teach that you do not have to be baptized, you can just say a prayer and ask God to forgive you and then go live any way you want, believing you will go to heaven when you die.

The Bible does not teach any of the above false doctrines! The devil wants you to believe you are "once save, always saved." People who teach these false doctrines are twisting the Scriptures to their own destruction (2 Peter 3:16). The people who teach and the people who practice these things are not in a right relationship with God. The Bible does not say that people will always be saved regardless of how they live their lives (especially those who willfully sin, see Hebrews 10:26-31). I challenge you to find one example of a Bible character who was disobedient to God, did not repent, maintained disobedience, and was approve by God. You won't find any such character in God's Word. God does not approve of disobedience.

Without Obedience, God Does Not Approve of Man

This is why it is necessary that you understand the importance of living an obedient life to God. Being obedient to God is important if you want to have a joyful relationship with Him. Otherwise, you are wasting your time and His. Do not bother, if you do not intend to be obedient.

John tells us we prove our love for God when we are obedient (1 John 2:3-6), and we have assurance that we "know" Him. Obedience is a milestone on the path of true worship. As I mentioned previously, we were created to glorify God. Our obedience brings glory (1 Peter 2:12). And James tells we deceive ourselves if we listen to the Word and do not obey (James 1:22-25).

Live an obedient life to God – one step and one day at a time, grow in your relationship.

Epilogue: Giving Your Best to God

As you follow the pattern for true worship laid out in this book, you will be drawn closer to God than ever before. Remember, a pure heart and proper attitude are necessary to obtain joy in your relationship with God. You must engage and *be active* in your relationship to find true joy.

As you give your best to God – based on His desires – and follow this roadmap which points to your best possible relationship with God, you will subconsciously achieve the following milestones:

Knowledge
Understanding
Wisdom
Love
Obedience
Trust
Faith
Extreme Joy (In God's Presence)

The ironic thing is that you won't need to focus on these milestones like a checklist to come into God's presence. Again, following the roadmap will allow you to achieve them as you walk with the Lord.

Knowledge, understanding, and wisdom are based on ***doctrine (truth)*** in scriptural authority. Once you obtain a solid foundation in how God expects you to worship Him, then you can move on to spiritual maturity (being ever conscious of God's presence and viewing life with Him as center). *Love, obedience, trust, faith, and extreme joy* are based on ***spirituality (spirit)***. See chapter seven on understanding the importance of worshipping God in spirit and in truth. Most specifically, meditate on the subsection on "doctrine versus spirituality." Remember, you can worship God in truth (according to doctrine) but fail to worship God in spirit (being ever conscious of God's presence and viewing life with Him as center). The only way for a Christian to have the relationship with God that He desires and He wants for us to enjoy is to understand and actively engage in true worship. That is worship the way God intended. True worship, or knowing God, is only possible when God is worshipped the way He desires.

This is the way to develop a closer relationship with God and experience the joy in worship that you have been seeking for so long.

Therefore, today is the beginning of the rest of your life, serving God with joy. *True* joy. Knowing you can withstand any hardship in your life because God is with you. Knowing your relationship with God is imperfect because you fall short, but also knowing that everyday God graciously has given you one more day to develop your relationship with Him. It is one more day for you to experience the joy that He intended for you to experience in this life, looking forward to eternity with Jesus, where the joy you will experience cannot be imagined in this life.

May God bless you richly as you endeavor to diligently seek His face (in spirit and in truth) and to draw closer to Him. May God be glorified and may you be overjoyed just like the Psalmist in 43:3.

"Then I will go to the altar of God, to God
– my exceeding joy..."

Appendix
20 Major Bible Events
by Book, Chapter and Date

"...according to the eternal purpose which He accomplished in Christ Jesus our Lord..."
(Ephesians 3:11)

1. Creation (4004 – 2091 BC)
   a. Genesis 1-5
2. Fall of Man
   a. Genesis 3
3. Flood
   a. Genesis 6-9
4. Scattering of the People
   a. Genesis 10-11
5. Patriarchs (2090 – 1875 BC)
   a. Genesis 11:27 – 50:26
   b. Job
6. Exodus (1875 – 1405 BC)
   a. Exodus (1875 – 1445 BC)
   b. Leviticus (1445 BC)
   c. Numbers 1-13 (1445/44 BC)
7. Wanderings (1444 – 1405 BC)
   a. Numbers 14 – Deuteronomy 34 (1444 – 1405 BC)
8. Conquest of the Land (1405 – 1380 BC)
   a. Joshua (1405 – 1380 BC)
9. Judges (1380 – 1045 BC)

a. Judges – 1 Samuel 7
b. Ruth

10. United Kingdom (1045 – 931 BC)
    a. 1 Samuel 8 – 1 Kings 11
    b. 1 Chronicles – 2 Chronicles 9
    c. Psalms
    d. Proverbs
    e. Ecclesiastes
    f. Song of Solomon
11. Divided Kingdom (931 – 722 BC)
    a. 1 Kings 12 – 2 Kings 25
    b. 2 Chronicles 10-36
    c. Obadiah (840 BC)
    d. Joel (835 BC)
    e. Jonah (760 BC)
    f. Amos (755 BC)
    g. Hosea (755 – 710 BC)
    h. Isaiah (740 – 680 BC)
    i. Micah (735 – 710 BC)
12. Judah Alone (722 – 605 BC)
    a. Nahum (663 – 612 BC)
    b. Zephaniah (630-625 BC)
    c. Jeremiah (627 – 580 BC)
    d. Habakkuk (607 BC)
13. Babylonian Captivity (606 – 536 BC)
    a. Daniel (605 – 536 BC)
    b. Ezekiel (592 – 570 BC)
14. Return (536 – 425 BC)
    a. Ezra 1-6 (538 – 515 BC)
    b. Haggai (520 BC)

c. Zechariah (520 – 470 BC)
d. Esther (483 – 473 BC)
e. Ezra 7-10 (457 BC)
f. Nehemiah (444 – 425 BC)
g. Malachi (432 – 425 BC)

15. Years of Silence (400 BC)
    a. Amos 8:11
16. Life of Christ (33 AD)
    a. Matthew
    b. Mark
    c. Luke
    d. John
17. Early Church (33 – 100 AD)
    a. Acts – Jude
18. Current Age
19. Return of Christ (?)
    a. Revelation 1-20
20. Dwelling with God
    a. Revelation 21-22

Bibliography

Ben. 2009. *Revelation.co.* January 5. Accessed August 31, 2018. http://www.revelation.co/2009/01/05/why-did-god-get-angry-at-the-tower-of-babel-people/.

Bible Journey. n.d. *The Bible Journey.* Accessed September 8, 2018. http://www.thebiblejourney.org/printer-friendly.php?page_id=619 .

Buseck, Craig von. 2018. *CBN.* August 31. Accessed August 31, 2018. http://www1.cbn.com/questions/what-are-the-three-parts-of-man.

2018. *Creation.com.* August 31. Accessed August 31, 2018. http://creation.com/noahs-flood-why.

Easley, Kendell H. 2002. *Understanding the Bible: A Book-by-Book Overview.* Nashville: Holman Bible Publishers.

Got Questions Ministries. 2018. *Got Questions.* August 31. Accessed August 31, 2018. https://www.gotquestions.org/why-did-God-create-us.html.

Got Questions. 2002-2018. *Who are the biblical patriarchs?* September 8. Accessed September

8, 2018. https://www.gotquestions.org/biblical-patriarchs.html.

2018. *Got Questions: Difference Between Soul and Spirit.* September 6. Accessed September 6, 2018. www.gotquestions.org .

Hafley, Larry. n.d. *Guardian of Truth.* Accessed September 25, 2018. http://www.truthmagazine.com/archives/volume39/GOT039251.html.

Henry, Gary. 2018. *Diligently Seeking God: Harder ... But Much Easier.* September 3. Accessed September 3, 2018. wordpoints.com.

Packer, J. I. 1973. *Knowing God.* Downers Grove, IL: InterVarsity Press.

Prince, Derek. 2007. Entering the Presence of God: Moving Beyond Praise and Thanksgiving to True Worship. New Kinsington: Whitaker House.

—. 2011. Set Apart for God: The Beautiful Secret of Holiness. New Kinsington, PA: Whitaker House.

The Bible Journey. 2018. *Judah Alone.* Accessed September 24, 2018. http://www.thebiblejourney.org/printer-friendly.php?page_id=619 .

—. 2018. *The Divided Kingdom Timeline.* Accessed September 24, 2018. http://www.thebiblejourney.org/printer-friendly.php?page_id=619.

Tozer, Aiden Wilson. 2007. *Mystery of the Holy Spirit.* Newberrt: Bridge-Logos.

—. 1948. The Pursuit of God: Three Spiritual Classics in One Volume. Chicago: The Moody Bible Institute of Chicago.

How to contact the author

I have prayed diligently for you. I have prayed this book has led you to an extremely ***joyful*** relationship with God the way He intended. I have prayed God would be ***glorified*** by your true worship as an individual and in the assembly.

If this book has encouraged or inspired you in some way, or you have questions about the content written herein, please give God the glory and contact me at

EarnestlyPursuingGOD@gmail.com.

All proceeds from this book will go to expanding the church of Christ and to godly saints in need.

www.ingramcontent.com/pod-product-compliance
Lightning Source LLC
LaVergne TN
LVHW051008080826
845145LV00009B/2511

* 9 7 8 1 9 4 7 6 2 2 3 0 2 *